THE DRUMS OF SILENCE

Kristiina Ehin

Translated by Ilmar Lehtpere

Kristiina Ehin is one of the most beloved poets in Estonia, a country where there is still widespread interest in poetry and a long tradition of great female poets. Winner of that country's most prestigious poetry prize for her work written during a year spent as a nature reserve warden on an uninhabited island, Ehin's work reflects the influence of the traditional Estonian folk song, which dates back over two thousand years. It is honest, uncompromising, deeply personal, universal, and utterly free from poetic fashion and convention.

❉

Kristiina was born in Rapla, Estonia, and has to date published four volumes of poetry in her native Estonian. She has also worked at a progressive school for children with special needs. Recently she has devoted her creative efforts to a collection of uniquely poetic short stories.

Ilmar Lehtpere had a bilingual upbringing in Estonian and English. His translations of Estonian poetry have appeared in various literary journals in Europe and America.

❉ ❉ ❉

KRISTIINA EHIN

The Drums of Silence

❀ ❀ ❀

Translated by Ilmar Lehtpere

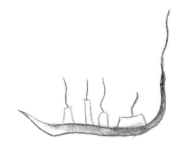

The Oleander Press

The Oleander Press Ltd
16 Orchard Street
Cambridge
CB1 1JT
England

ISBN 0-906672-740
ISBN 978-906672-747

Cover illustration by Kristiina Ehin
Cover design by Peter Ducker

Typeset by BookType
Printed and bound in Great Britain

ACKNOWLEDGEMENTS

Some of these translations first appeared in the following journals:
Poetry Ireland Review, *The Stinging Fly*, *Cyphers* and *Crannóg*

This translation is published with the support of a Traducta
grant from the Cultural Endowment of Estonia.

CONTENTS

the clustered berries of my loving
russet and heavy

the birds for company

❁

INTRODUCTION

Kristiina Ehin is one of the most beloved poets in Estonia, a country where there is still widespread interest in poetry. She was born in Rapla, Estonia in 1977. Her parents are both also well-known poets and translators. She has an M.A. in Comparative Folklore from Tartu University, and to date has published four volumes of poetry. The latest, which won Estonia's most prestigious poetry prize, was written during a year spent as a nature reserve warden on an otherwise uninhabited island off Estonia's north coast. She has also worked at a progressive school for children with special needs, using the creative, healing power of fairy tales to help children who would not be able to cope at a conventional school. Recently she has been devoting her creative efforts to prose as well, and the result is a collection of uniquely poetic short stories.

Kristiina is the latest in a long line of great female poets in Estonia stretching back to the folk tradition. The form of traditional Estonian folk song, highly alliterative trochaic tetrametre, also known as Kalevala metre, is certainly two thousand years old. The vast majority of traditional Estonian folk songs were composed and sung by women. Among the criteria these traditional singers were judged by was their improvisation skills – their ability to spontaneously create songs to suit the occasion. Kristiina regards these traditional singers as role models. The oral folk tradition in Estonia survived well into the twentieth century, and there is a vast body of material in the archives which presents a distinctly female view of Estonian folk culture and folk history. She also has a deep affinity for the Finno-Ugric minorities (Estonia's close relations) in Russia, for whom the Soviet Union has never really ended, and has travelled extensively among the Udmurts, Mari, Khanty and Mansi. She has woven the mythology and folklore of these peoples into her own work.

In the world of formal literature as well, women have always set the tone, beginning in the nineteenth century with Lydia Koidula, and continuing in the twentieth century with Marie Under, Betti Alver, Kersti Merilaas, Viivi Luik and Doris Kareva, to name but a few. And now Kristiina Ehin. Kristiina's very distinctive poetry speaks for itself. It is honest, uncompromising, deeply personal, universal, and utterly free from poetic fashion and convention. Her poetry spans centuries, millennia. It is at once modern and primeval.

For Estonian poets, their native tongue is a blessing because it is a wonderfully expressive and flexible tool. The complex grammatical structure with its plethora of inflections – there are fourteen cases – means that a word's function is identified by its ending and not its position in the sentence. There are almost no prepositions and only a handful of postpositions, as this function is fulfilled by the case endings. This makes word order almost totally free, and allows for highly nuanced expression. And even the most commonplace concepts are often expressed in images – "next to", for example, is "kõrval" in Estonian, and literally means "at the ear (of)"; "juures"– literally, "in the root (of)" – means "at". But unfortunately Estonian poets have a very small potential audience for their work – there are only one million speakers of Estonian, and although some Estonian poets achieve sales figures their counterparts in much larger countries could only dream of, they remain undeservedly unknown on the international scene. In Western Europe and North America there is often a lack of interest in the poetry of small nations, even though these nations tend to have a very lively poetic culture. This is partly due to the fact that there is also a great lack of translators who have sufficient command of these languages. Hopefully, this volume of poems by a truly great poet will begin to correct the balance.

hair grey with youth

*

you sit at your table and write

I grow into your room
like a yellow blossomed thorny flower
mercilessly
together with the sun
I tell fairy tales
of the time I grew up in the mountains
of the orchids my sisters
of the tornado my brother

your pencil drops
your eyelids tremble
how did I get here?

*

Come what will
young horse chestnuts will turn black with decay
and the first hailstones will catch us joyfully
and not melt on the tongue
come what will
evening will tear itself loose from day's hands
and slide down
along night's darkening slope

you learn a foreign language
and chirp the dark sap of your feelings out
but the tall trees of my childhood
have rolled up their swings
and are fleeing towards the sea
come what may

*

this room –
lengths of wallpaper from Russian times
scraping against the here and now of our glances
age old floor boards
against the soles of our feet hot with youth
how are you to find yourself between
the varnished ceiling
and dusty stairs of this house

I haven't believed mirrors for a long time now

every one of them yearns for a different me
wanting to touch the sun's redness in my cheeks
with its glassy hand

only the peaceful bright green river
of my childhood
showed a reflection I felt was my own –
it moved even when I didn't
it showed tremors of laughter
and the habit of tears to dry quickly
or fall lightly and boldly
into their own reflection

the days flow slowly
like a stream torpid from waiting
or quickly like rapids when
I feel the swirling cascade of your eyes before me
doors open and close again
on the plastic framed window ledge
the queen sits and sews

three drops of blood fall onto the snow

*

a hot day in Brezhnev's time
and I still just a little girl
in a blue cotton print skirt
flee through the yellow corn field
from the big people's big birthday
where the aspic melted on long party tables
and my sisters and cousins had disappeared
into peals of laughter from the hammock and berry bushes

and then
suddenly I come
to a deserted country house

in a broken box I find a slender pipe
that smells of old men
even older than grandfather
a black sweet bitter pipe from between the lips
of a frighteningly old sick man maybe
already dead

it fitted into my pocket and all evening
swinging nodding off eating strawberry cake
I felt its lovely
black soothing stem
in my sweaty palm

*

a girl with big hurrying night eyes
the harbours of her heart bustling
ships of promises setting out
on a long voyage

you took a girl got a woman
you took a boy got a man
you took a woman got an old crone
you took a man got an old codger

where do rivers begin
from somebody's tears
where do garlands begin
from the first two flowers
where do songs come from
the way footprints are left
in the green morning grass

how did the stars come into being
my sister night wanted to take a husband
I took the beads from round my neck
to adorn her

*

youth tasting of sesame
is strung around your neck
you caress the trees
reel down the steps
tremors of happiness on your shoulders
you quell the gate as you open your thirst
near the woodpile
tubs filled to the brim
with the melted waters
of October

you are still a child of the city
through and through
you envy your grandmothers' bright white
confirmation dresses
you don't know where to hide your long hair
who to share the flush of joy in your cheeks with
is everything really only
the blind rhythm of your feet
a dance of yellowed leaves
from one new-moon morning to the next

*

I know the hour
when many-coloured carpets rest on the floor
and long benches wait for visitors
when fortune flowers
and the grey heifer calf born this spring
is still asleep
our rooms and sheds and stables
smell of split boards
this house is still young
we are still young
summers yet unborn
glisten in our eyes
and there
are so many places
in this timbered house
where no one
has been able to make a nest yet

silver coins don't tarnish
labour pains don't kill
the gateposts shine at night
the springs of Harju steam
in the mossy marsh of the womb
my daughters swayed
and my sons climbed out
of the rusty bog water
where are the grandmothers
they are already dead
where are the grandfathers
they are already dead
where is your silk hatband
and your silver ring
lost in the move
on the heavy cartload that took us to town
but the heavy load remained

the whole heavy load remained on the heart
meadows blazing with summer flowers
yuletide apparitions
the hollow hours struck by the old wall clock
and letters as if from another world
and photographs of all those grown-ups
and all those linden trees
that had once been children
their branches full of light green blossoms

tunes that carried my heart

1.

it is night
king's son
far away the towers of your castle
conquer the morning sky
but you say
that you know no lovelier dawn than me in your hands

ahhh

I am the unbelievers' brood of vipers
I am the darling of whisperings and yet the only one
not permitted to take you seriously
you kindle a flame in my eyes
as if the me of dreams had forgotten herself
as if the night fog and the raindrops on my cheek
had done their work

2.

I was born at midsummer
and will die at midsummer
but just now I am celebrating a wedding
whirling in the rustling of my gown around
my
still slender waist
plaited hair flying in the wind
where the town ends
where the great forest begins

I am up all night
to hear and to listen to
tunes that carried my heart
in an old boat of linden wood
down the holy river

what riverbanks did it glide to
what rushes did it drift to
in what ancient country
on what a morning

ahhh

hands sought hands
surge led on to surge
white birches bent over
hair grey with youth

a devil's dozen miles
I have walked in the night
through the forest where you can but pray
looking for the morning
that vowed
to come no more

*

your heart falls into my lap
like a big unhappy onion
there's a full moon tonight
the windows creak
agonizingly
above our heads
the stars crackle
like fires on marsh islands

even so closeness is so
elusive
far away may be too far
a foreign land too foreign
there isn't much time
there isn't much choice
we haven't the heart to spill
a single drop of the blood of parting

that's why you can't turn
your gaze from the hollows of your hands
that's why you can't disappear
like a horse bolting
over the dry
moorland

*

even now the fog comes to howl at my door
to wail to dream
and create us anew

the soles of the oaks reach far under ground

in a dream I saw two moons
one big sphere and another even bigger one

on that clear night
the first belonged to everyone
and the second was
my very own moon – the beautiful eye of a dinosaur
your vanished face
through which I saw into myself

*

youth flows slowly out of the lakes of my eyes
will you make it in time to drink from them
the leaves are already falling from this summer's trees
and from this summer's trees
even my loving words
are dropping off

with my sandals in my bag I go down into the valley
the night air under my lapels
and I wide awake
ever the loser and scorcher of new wings

*

already rowan leaves are sprouting
sturdy trees speaking sweet words
in the ferment of the night

you are asleep
work and money
silence your days
the moon and stars
would bloody your heart

I rile you
I am dangerously sharp and fresh
I wake with the sun
smell the blades of grass in the garden
touch the splashes of light
and go my own way

*

your drums are silent
you hurry home and to school
through the gentle violet morning
over the anemone white day
through parks
smelling
of the sap of maples

through cawing crows and
bloodstains
through white silence
and the midnight of cats fighting
you have yet to go

*

the warmish February tricks you
with its muddy main street
even the pedestrian crossing mocks you

don't believe it

in the darkest street
in the greyest house
behind the faded curtain
I sit
happy as a precious stone in the palm of a poor child

look for me
eternal wanderer
if there is still a veranda in your blood
if your heart is as strong as a climbing rose
and roving swarms of stars
meet in your eyes

*

the moon howls
over my roof
the moon howls
and legs die

the moon is making a heavy rope
from the hair of a corpse
and is coming
down
tonight

the moon summons my bones
and through the bone calls out

the moon pulls us about
howls and demands
a keg of strong drink

a cadaverous old woman
wanting old-fashioned friendship
and a remedy for her loneliness

for too long now she has felt with her body
how light rushes
for too long now emptiness
has been lapping against
the dry shores of her imagination

they stood under a slanted roof

dolls with tears in their eyes fall
from the window ledge into the night
what could the dream mean
I was careering through the forest
and the cars were speeding towards me
head-on
how did I stay on the road

a little girl
I don't remember why
later danced and I danced along
so eerie all around and the swarm of people
who weren't dancing
just watching
they stood
under a slanted roof
and watched us like a film
they stood under a slanted roof
and didn't see how the clouds were fleeing

*

bluish-green spring beside me
so snow afflicted
with lips so cracked
bluish-green spring
my bright unsettled friend
takes hold of my sleepy hand
and leads me to see how
the night tears up its dress of clouds
and the moon appears before me
stark naked
stripped bare
like a child who doesn't demand anything more
and wonders before sleep
what will become of us after we die

land of tree worshippers

tidings of St George's night

for nineteen thousand silver marks
my country was sold
I saw dreadful things
amid the rushes in Saaremaa

the ring around the last stronghold
drew tighter
and 13 black ravens flew cawing
towards Livonia

I am the envoy of fate
the wretched witness
who must affix the dying screams
of her own brothers onto paper

658 winters I have been on the road
rough paper against my warm body
but my horse is old and frail
and my coat too much the colour of the land
for anyone to take heed of
how terror-stricken the horses whinnied
as the cross lashed out
how coldly the silver coins rang
in the Danish king's pocket

woman of gold

1.

You took great pains with me
sculpting and shaping
polishing and chanting spells
honing a greater beauty
conjuring a sleeker one

my eyes let sparks fly
mocking and fire-hot –
what do you want to make of me
an ornament
a goddess?

you gathered up the fathers' gold
gathered up six brothers' gold
gold for a face O
silver for its beauty O

ouch!

why didn't I tell you
you're wasting your time
not gold
but joy
will set my form
aglow like a goddess
not silver
but a quiet evening
can make my body radiant with beauty
and so it is
so it is forever
with great-grandmothers mothers and daughters
one woman gives life to another
passes on her own beauty to her
in blood and pain

your gold
is the husk
we shake off with a laugh
there's no point in shaping and sculpting
forgive me
you're wasting your time
one day I'll be dried up and wrinkled anyway

but never bowed

  2.

men make a woman
perhaps they really do
a good man
puts a woman out to grow like woundwort

how is she not to grow into a woman then
when the sun makes its sixteenth yearly ring
how is a child not to be brought into the world then
when the moon's belly has swelled lopsided
for the three hundredth time

long so long are the years
but
life is fleeting

don't construct a woman
rather make her a house
of chippings and swan bone
make it of everything you have
and then
saw the windows in deep
so the sun can find its way in

*

a girl
not from the cover of a magazine
not from the television
not from the stage
an ordinary girl
this evening in her room

she alters and emerges from her shell
she changes her skin
slowly and painfully
she gets her spirit ready

that's why
she's the very one
this evening
the fairest
in all the land

*

the first riddle touches on the senses
the apple tree lined border of a yard
that I know even in pitch-darkness

the second touches on dreaming
belief that easily fades

the third is
a voiceless cry

the fourth
a bewitched knife in a younger brother's hand
and the blade knows
how the older brother fares

the fifth
the hour you are to come
neither walking nor riding
neither naked nor clothed

the sixth
the last petal of justice
that still will not fall

*

my brother is going off to war
this sultry morning
he wanted to
he wanted to so much
he is riding off joyfully
and the bright clouds
are chasing after him

my hair is the colour of meadowsweet
and the day has put blood in my cheeks
and yet and yet
my strong hands have no strength
to hold him back

ravisher of women

you are a man of the north
norseman of the storms
old scars roam along your muscled flesh
and your swords are as heavy as islands in the sea

my spell caught you by the hair
under a big stone
so I could study you
so I could walk round you
with the sun and against the sun
how you thrash about
how you howl
even the sun to setting

on a long and starry night
I observe you handsome viking
your eyelids fall shut
like the gates of a stronghold
in what runes
can your dreams be read?
half man half beast
my captive

*

my limbs metamorphose
fur grows on my beautiful body
in my mouth I feel teeth like clear death
all my listless love of peace supplanted by an agile thirst for blood

in the distance I hear the howling of my grey kin
I feel the rough touch of their grey snouts
on my young skin

I wanted to live with them
howl at the moon and suckle cubs –

but they won't have me as one of their own
for my gnarled human nature
still shows in my eyes

*

whatever I can imagine already is –
even love where hearts
call to each other like berry pickers in the forest –
and the huge momentum of the swing
creaking and squeaking in the night
wheeling over the bar
the sweat of beauty and fear in my palms
the taste of blood in my mouth

and spirits from a second
a hundred and third
a coming and going world
who knock and walk and open and close doors
but still
do not dare to step into the pure circle of my sight
and old people who for some unexplainable reason are
younger than the young
and children and dogs
that simply no one has the heart to raise too well
the sweet strawberry glade I found in a dream
and hands
that unite

*

this is your big rosy-cheeked life
rolling past
life like an apple

the daring gather twigs for the fire
round the old witch's house
twigs and frozen berries

sea holidays
and every shallow puddle
has closed its clear summer eyes
in a film of ice

what remains is life like an apple
life like a ripe autumn apple
life that hasn't yet rolled past

stealthily very stealthily
I drop its seeds on the ground
to find the way back from
where everyone has strayed

*

the afternoon sun shines on the backs of our heads
as we bend down under the oxen yoke
of our lives
faithful shadows
black as the harness
salty and warm from the evening sun
your eyes – dark as gratitude

in voices hoarse with sleep
we whisper dreamy words
windows drip with rain
the wind rattles in the staircase
and the last leaves fall rustling into the well

what are we to believe then
here in this land of tree worshippers
where the pulpits still flow with spilt blood
blood
the tree gods were without

*

the old linden at Pärlijõgi
persevered for two hundred summers
then one morning
the wind blew the mist from the meadow

you saw a bolt of lightning cleave the linden
at that moment for the very first time
your daughter gave a start below your heart

you sat on the faeries' stone
pale and uneasy
for days on end you watched the frogs spawning
in the dusky haymaking time
you breathed the bright evening seeds
deep into your soul

the old linden at Pärlijõgi
persevered for two hundred summers
until for the very first time
your daughter gave a start below your heart

*

I don't believe in any fairy tales other
than life itself
for every prince and his ardent kisses
is less than a stone's throw away from me

and the faeries live in the next room
we consort with each other
and we often burst out laughing
about other humans' disbelief

but how can I persuade you that
the world beneath the sky is full of wonder
why do you look at me again so warily
and walk around with such a sullen look

*

the time is at hand
when the world cracks
when the sap flows down the birch
and everything you knew
slowly falls apart

the time is at hand
when you dance your ungainly dance
rub your hips against your shadow
see with the soles of your feet
hear with your tongue
feel the leaves falling beyond the hills

the time is at hand
when the iron door of your heart is open
earthen tiles will not burn
the handrail will not waver
you can see what mineral you're made of
what plain water
what rarefied air

*

lonely forest lakes
I leave behind
patches of snow melt on the hillsides
stone walls in the countryside
and roofs that have flown their own way in a fierce wind
footprints of a twirling dance
stay
and the lovely habit of human hands to clasp into full swing

wind chases the water
in the puddles in the ditches
at the bend of the river in the heart of night
two figures have stopped
but the river doesn't stop
two figures stand
but the river wanders
two children of man endured and recovered
but the river knew
it would stay behind
to carry and to listen

new men and women I leave behind me
to tremble with freedom and grow old
new houses and an old very old house's windows facing
the sun
new girls and new gravestones
new boys and new coffins
new states
and old
very old peoples
new computers
and the last breaths drawn by ancient kindred clans
new clothes and new banknotes
new codes and bones
new stars and windfalls

and old very old
love
like a needle in a frosty morning haystack
that human fingers fervently seek

endless mountains of rubbish
I leave behind
even in the other world I feel my own consumer life
the smell
of plastic bags shiny paper and plastic containers burning
acrid reek penetrates the elements and the eyes
women still reputed to be weak I leave
behind me
wealth tearing men to shreds
seconds lashing on the shoulders of those destitute of time

Death the fellow with the worn out cap
comes wearily from his blood-soaked work and
Life blossoming and blithe
stays to wait for him at the window

*

a gunman stands in the yard
asks where is your husband?
announces you have two hours time
and then...
what will I bundle together?
my heart is tightening
what will I tell the children?
two hours
and then?
who will milk my mooing cows
should I ask god?
the sun is waking on the field
slow and reddening
who can I hope to get help from?
should I ask the farmhand?
the sun is waking on the field
blood-red
the children and bundled belongings onto the cart
oh they are fiendish brutes!
at the edge of the forest my husband's
despair
stays behind to watch us go

*

a giant airplane
a boeing 757
fell in love with a grey heron
oh how it wanted
to fly over the marsh
where the heron stood
on a rough stump
slender legs
so thin and long
eyes half shut within itself
feathers the colourless colour of dreams
to see for a moment the black of its wings
the sharp brushstroke of its open beak
oh how it wanted
to set down its hurrying passengers
to leave its tedious everyday work
and swoop down to the heron
to twirl and to dance
to whirl wildly
on the rusty bog
its oh so bright and shining body
yearning to feel the nearness of bird feathers
to fall asleep wing in wing
against the heron's colourless colour of dreams

and then it would whisper to the heron
wake up heron
look how full of fiery stars
the sky is
up there I only felt
the warmth of the fuel
the call to hurtle on

the clustered berries of my loving
russet and heavy

*

you went looking for your eyes
in Siberia's deep rivers
the endless tundra sang your soul bare
the forests silenced your eyes into mossy softness
and with your fingers you scratched
the budding antlers of reindeer calves furtively born

is that why
you know how to touch
my soul so easily
without drowning
in the legendary sea of my dreaming eyes?

you drank warm blood
from the neck of a sacrificial animal
spoke to no one for months
but trees and songbirds

is that why
you can observe me with interest in a café
the way you would look at
flaming red clouds of an evening?

you have slept three hundred miles away
from the nearest town
between two hills of snow
alone
your feet bleeding
your compass lost
and your fire iron broken

is that why
you are dark and forever unfilled
like the night?

*

I smell you at the crossroads in the heart of night
to let my lungs revive
I smell you
meateater and trail stalker

there is the scent of the sky
and a beard growing

just as I thought

I scent the glistening lakes of your eyes
that are accustomed to quenching thirst and cooling
I scent how clean and fertile are the fields of your dreams
light and warm the soil of your wishes
and how happy your mother was giving birth to you

oh how dangerous to be so near
now you can't keep your eyes off
I want to flee
but for that this moment is
too great a wonder
and far away is every reason
why we shouldn't...

fidelity – rough as a man's cheek
raw meat that draws you close
a trail that remains
a trail that can't be abandoned

*

the red hawthorn berries of my cheeks
against the sallow pride of your mortality
how did I notice your eyes in the sea of people?

we were suddenly the only visitors in the art building
the rooms void of people
full of feelings
the storm bell high above
or rather deep within us?

the wind the wind
wants to catch us
howl along housing
unloose clothing off hooks
have fingers cling to fingers
hold on to the only thing that can't be held on to – life
so beautiful and against all reason

the wind fills our sleeves and we fly away
leaving our shadows behind on the ground –
the lightest and heaviest of gravestones

*

when you come dangerously close
the garden is full of slippery snow
on the dark eaves a rook croaks
its vanishing youth
its rough gutteral voice lingers
to finish this day
the last snow before the warm spring
lingers to begin our life

the look in your brown eyes
is like tree-bark
that the sun seeps through
and your mouth melts the last flakes of fear
from my lips

below my chin
on my throat
there is an everlasting light spot
from my water lily white years
and no desire
or touch that makes me blush all over
can wipe it away
it isn't snow and so it won't melt
even in warmth such as this

when the garden is full of slippery snow
and two ugly ducklings
notice themselves
in the mirror of each other's eyes

on the way to Siberia

1.

when we arrived
Izhkar itself glowed to meet us in the evening sun
the rising fever of our love
made us restless
and gave us time
made everything light
and heavy

in a café a gold-toothed seller sold
us sweet black tea
and the last curd cake
which lay between us on the table
hard and distant like the moon

and already I'm asleep on the veranda
on the soft flowered pillows of your childhood home
on my sun-tanned hands
and you slip through two living-rooms
to talk to me again
of books and train times
and again to twirl between your fingers my sleek
hair
never entangled by colours
or subject to curls

and suddenly you are entirely blanketed in my hair
and our bodies entwine
into the wordless grace of passion and peace
into endless beginning
our mouths close
innocence and death
tremble in my nostrils
innocence and death
vibrate in your fingers

what is real in this
mortal life
what is lasting
in this world falling like a maple leaf?

2.

autumn equinox on the Surgut train
we were like a compartment full of gold kopecks
cheerful sparkling tinkle fell from us all around
the chiming hung in the air
ringing at the rails
our clotted grown-up wisdom
melted and shimmered

airy and easy
our talk over the table
the long journey and love
gave us time

slumbering houses
gardens drowning in apples
flee past
and a hundred million fairy tales
that will never be fulfilled
but stay to fill
the depths of the heart

3.

two days later we were suddenly superfluous
our glances strayed along the muddy town
soaked through
we sat in the snack bar
and didn't see through each other's city faces

4.

out in the country again
a piece of the curd cake moon bitten off and swallowed
we are in a forest that is spoken to
we are believers like the mist
light as yellow leaves
fragile as the evening sun
we are in a forest that has been spoken to
a forest where neither good nor evil grows
where everything is intertwined
life birth death and life again
I pull you down onto the moss
and we stretch out on the fallen leaves
your fingers dig wells in the desert hues of my hair
how many new lives are reflected
in the depths of our eyes?

5.

the storm lifted us up high
down below in the taiga colourful kerchiefs remained to cheer
women and men remained to live their own life
so beautiful and harsh
woodpeckers to rap
at the silky sides of birches
squirrels to climb
to the tops of cedars

we flew drawn by reindeer
high low
even higher
lower
is that why these strange shivers
are running up and down
along my spine?

*

I came dancing into Moscow
a ravished enraptured woman
the thrilling dark of the metro
kindled a never before known
fire in my eyes

now I know how hands can cling to hands
and feet rush so lightly without quickening
and hands stroke beggars' hats

in the morning in Pskov antennae were slumped sideways
from nights of loving

it's going to be a lovely clear day

you push your barrel organ out to work
music begins to seep out
between my fingers
birch trees fling gold
into the room
our figures are black
black
only for the moment we are human bees
sucking by chance on life's honeycomb
fish walking in the air
a very special breed...

*

I want to be a night bird
who on March evenings such as this
goes into your tree-trunk to doze
and in the heart of night
and in the heart of night
can't but kiss your dark acorns
your roots and branches murmur indifference
I forget human speech
seeking in the rustling of leaves
words
on tiptoe at the cliff-edge of silence
I listen to the heart
in which life exults
behind the dusky bark of muteness

*

magnanimous night
the gentle fever of sweet scent
in your hair
the tender remembrance
of the sun on your cheeks
such a night
where the one who doesn't know how to answer
has to kiss the questioner

it still isn't winter yet
it's a dark sooty evening
and my eyes have contracted into black cannon shot

life bigger than death is in your eyes and
and a great many
questions heavy as eider-down

*

the clustered berries of my loving
russet and heavy
rain outside hones the rounded night
on the stairs the dice of leaving roll
who whom
goblets of currant wine on the veranda
from the back of your eyes I roll signs of sympathy
I roll joy and breaths yet to be gasped

I flit into the night like a just awakened bat

roll on roll on black dice of leaving
let the rain outside do its work
the clustered berries of my loving
russet and heavy

*

call love to mind

when the wind steps on
the ice sharp stairs and breathes

call love to mind

when storm lanterns immortalize the silence
and old pine tree trunks
smell of resin

call love to mind

when the last splashes of sun forget themselves
in the grey-brown river of your eyes

call love to mind

when all at once the evening air gives
every bygone day a name
and you run to the stairs
struck dumb with a thirst for life

*

when the eaves are dripping
but it still isn't spring yet
the earrings in my boxes wake
and silk scarves rustle impatiently
against my cupboard doors

there's a luminous silence
in the ball of my eye
luminous
quivering
up to my knees in sunlight
I push my heart's lightsome
little boat
free from the muddy shore

the birds for company

*

it is a time you can see
through a dozen forests
trees as bare as a soul
woods barren of berries and mercies

snow descended from eternity
on this and the far side of seeing
I touched a shadow
that appeared before me
who knows where from

I stroked its dark
deep sunken cheeks
its eyeless eye-sockets

if you were to come to life
I would have to go
or we would go together
to where the snowstorm is coming from
to where it is going

*

to walk and to walk my own road
to speak to death and you
my days break off rumbling
from life's crags
and thoughts those free elusive
swallows
fly hither and thither
looking for food from feelings

to walk and to walk my own road
to speak to death and you
sleep's retina throbbing
at the edge of waking
so fleeting is the day
that I can scarcely give it a name

to walk and to walk my own road
to speak to death and you
the whole of the cold spring day
I look in the grass
for a big rust-coloured key
that would unlock
the home teetering and mouldering
at the edge of this land and the world
the only home that might befit us

*

down below the city growls
the city you can flee to
from the deep silence
within you

the endless city
no one walks through anymore
avenues lined with beeches
that would like to flee
to be floors and boats
and not have to stand
on the banks of this river of speed
with their leaves sheltering
the last breathful of air
to clean with their shoots new districts
fumes
blood circulation
and the steep shores of sincerity

down below the city growls
where can I hide my own deep silence
away from it?

*

in a dream
I saw a ticket booth
at a bus stop where
birds' feathers were sold instead of tickets
and the seller was...
an old man
with the early spring sun in his eyes

and for you young lady...
he said slowly
and took from somewhere next to the door
where there might have been
a bin and a broom
one more feather
a white plume
light and as tall
as himself

I paid and went
in dream's muddy buses
no notion of waking
no fear of inspection

*

fog appears imperceptibly
ships have set sail
together with white flocks of swans
frozen gravel crunches
at the gate
and the house plants draw back
shivering away from the windows

you don't know what to write about
on this morning of stillness
slowly shifting into evening
where thoughts rush out ahead of words
today you don't want to find
images of solitude
paint silence
or rush breathlessly headlong to meet the future

the day lingers
and it's gone
suddenly even the maps are frozen solid

*

March evenings grow red
on my brow
the cranes' frail shadows
silently clap
the rags of their wings
the moon roves round
in its check cosmos
your radio waves
go through me
standing alone here
at the edge of the world's die
in my soul
the low drums
of silence

and so spring is ready
ripe for falling from the black trees
like melting snow

to fear and to dare

the hollows of your hands sandy
you eye me shyly
the dancers are far away now
the flowing water reflecting fiddle tunes

you arrive back at your hotel
and for half the night before falling asleep
you think that you did after all dare
to touch my cheeks
and push the hair away
with both hands

man and bird

on your back
is written "man"
I read it so I don't forget
icicles drip and
the hall door is open
so we can cry
our laughter out

spring came
over our feathered shoulders
and our hearts were kindled aflame like
cleansing spring fires

these are the stones
we jump along
and neither of us falls
for we know how to use wings
these are my own life-lined hands
that mix food for the birds

when you drew away
over the beautiful muddy fields
I had the birds for company
you had sold a little patch
of your endless sea
and we were richer
than ever before

*

You went and the lighthouse
was left hanging toward the sky
the nailheads of the stars
fast in the ceiling
of the sky

you went and the moon
was left broken
like half of a ring

I stand on the shore
old flight tickets in my pockets
and dog food

I stand on the shore my back to the heavy wind
the same wind
blowing in your face

*

there are cracks in my blue dress
like in my light brown lips
the sea wind carries the last seeds of evening
and flocks of swans disappear behind the distant islets

two seagulls sit on my tower step
and the smaller one is you
broken beaked
with a sullen look

you say those egg shells will never be
there will never be cheeping of fledglings or their first flight
over countryside white with frost

– and yet you come every morning
to eat from my hand
and every evening to drink the ice melting
from my windows

*

as flesh and blood I rush breathlessly through the land
at night I sink down keeled over on the shores of my own life
in the storm the lighthouses resound
the sea provides me with dreams
and suddenly it seems
as if all the drops of water are coins
jingling all the world's wealth
against the poor old stones
everything can be sold off
but this sea of coins will never end
everything can be bought up
but still there will be this money of the restless seas left over

the whole of Marianas Trench full
a whole oceanful of money
between America and Eurasia
whole shoalfuls of coins
and silvery foam marks
sunken steamers' smokestacks
filled to overflowing with gold kopecks
turbine ships and lightships full of dollars
storm bells' tin clappers stopped up with tin thalers

and the gold of sunsets on the ocean
really is gold
and the path of the moon on the ocean is genuine silver for every onlooker
and robber
and runner and walker

and the fishermen's nets are suddenly full of real riches
solemnly the sea creatures watch
them with their sparkling diamond eyes

with a shovel gold is turned out of the sunset
with a crowbar silver prised out of the moonlight
with trembling fingers the fishes' diamond solemn eyes plucked out

and I still asleep keeled over on life's shore
and suddenly it seems as if there is no point
in the breathless headlong rush of my waking
such heavy water such valuable treasures of the sea
cannot be rippled by the wind
lifted by the hand
or carried far and wide by ships

in the storm the lighthouses resound

after the storm

in the morning I gather from the shore
slivers of broken bottles voidex containers
vodka vera bottles
jars still sloshing and smelling
of the marinade of shashlik long since devoured
trodden-on sunglasses
beach radio batteries
I gather bon aquas and evians
soft drink caps and beer cans
so much so much so much
plastic and metal and glass
and not a single ring
and not a solitary
cup with a golden handle

I gather and gather and gather
on this clear morning
into a black rubbish bag
hands and feet of dolls from soviet times
the rubber head of a baby penguin
a Russian border guard hat
so small?
was he still a child?
bits of foam rubber light as butterflies
flee from between my hands numb with cold
not a single cup
not a single ring
but so many other things

an inflatable rubber woman
meant to be used
in the water? while swimming?
full of holes like cheese
breasts airlessly drooping
toothless mouth unable to scream invitingly open
under her eyelids daubed with blue
still bluer eyes filled with the emptiness of being used
What sort of man
cuddled you and used you
before the storm
brought you here in its embrace

into this clear morning's big black rubbish bag

I tear the filmy plastic off my delicate beach roses
the leafless thorny branches
need to be cleared before the heavy spring winds
blow on the still unopened buds
I clear them so my proud roses need not grow
through this film of plastic flown here from who knows where
to clasp fawning and fluttering
to the thorny branches

my hands are pricked and punctured
and the morning ends
but at sunset I run home
fingers heavy with rings
hands bent round a cup

*

dreams are like deer
shy and self-contained
I am a hunter on the foggy shore of dreams
a hunter who never takes aim
but never takes
her eyes off

on the shore of death's great white lake
life began
every morning we crushed the glowing red bilberries into jam
and cleaned the wild mushrooms

two dark rivers of life flowed into the lake
and one
only one came out

on the foggy shore of dreams
I am a hunter who never takes
her eyes off

Printed in Great Britain
by Amazon